Gray Whale Migration

by Grace Hansen

Abdo
ANIMAL MIGRATION
Kids

Abdo Kids Jumbo is an Imprint of Abdo Kids
abdobooks.com

abdobooks.com

Published by Abdo Kids, a division of ABDO, P.O. Box 398166, Minneapolis, Minnesota 55439.

Printed in the United States of America, North Mankato, Minnesota.

052020

092020

THIS BOOK CONTAINS RECYCLED MATERIALS

Photo Credits: Alamy, BluePlanet Archive, iStock, Minden Pictures, Shutterstock

Production Contributors: Teddy Borth, Jennie Forsberg, Grace Hansen
Design Contributors: Dorothy Toth, Pakou Moua

Library of Congress Control Number: 2019956491

Publisher's Cataloging-in-Publication Data

Names: Hansen, Grace, author.

Title: Gray whale migration / by Grace Hansen

Description: Minneapolis, Minnesota : Abdo Kids, 2021 | Series: Animal migration | Includes online resources and index.

Identifiers: ISBN 9781098202330 (lib. bdg.) | ISBN 9781098203313 (ebook) | ISBN 9781098203801 (Read-to-Me ebook)

Subjects: LCSH: Gray whale--Juvenile literature. | Gray whale--Behavior--Juvenile literature. | Animal migration--Juvenile literature. | Animal migration--Climatic factors--Juvenile literature.

Classification: DDC 599.522--dc23

Table of Contents

Gray Whales

Gray whales live in the Pacific and Atlantic Oceans. One large population lives in the eastern Pacific Ocean.

South for the Winter

Eastern Pacific gray whales live off the coast of Alaska. There are around 24,000 individuals in the group. Each October, these whales start **migrating** south toward Mexico.

Alaska
Mexico

Gray whales can **migrate** around 75 miles (121 km) a day. In one year, they will travel about 13,000 miles (21,000 km). This is believed to be the longest migration of any **mammal**.

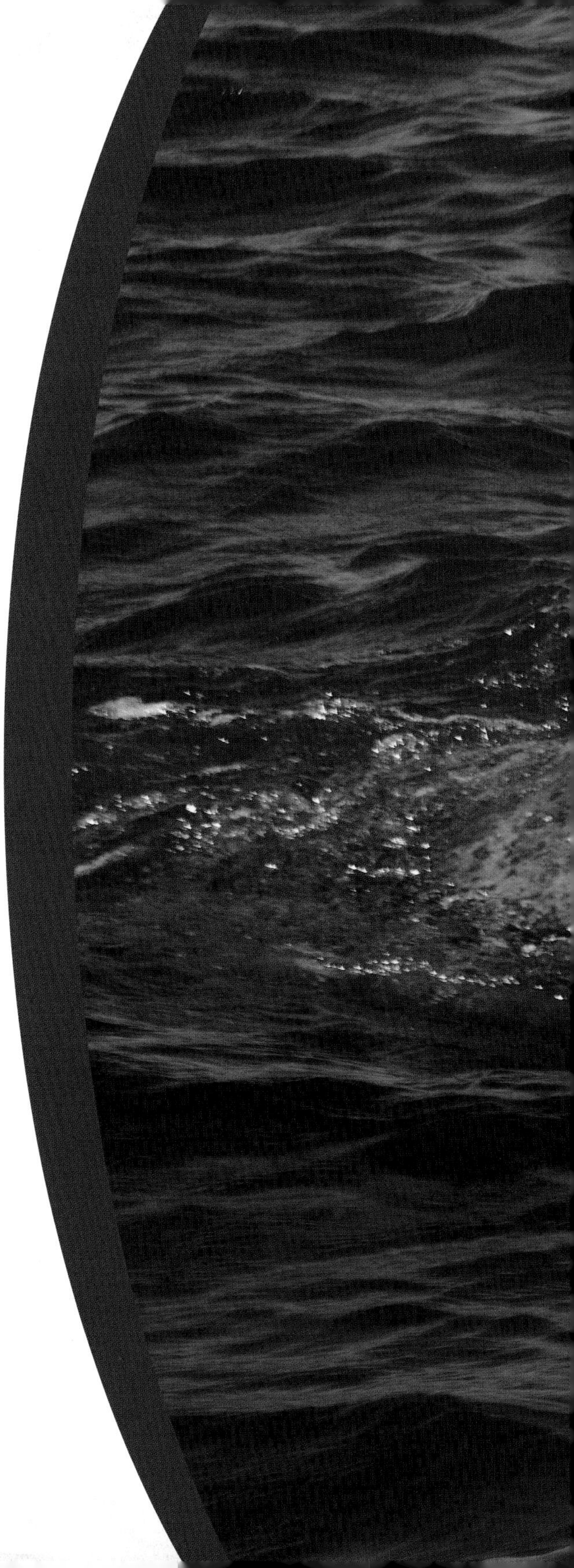

The whales make it to Mexico by late December. The water is warmer off the coast of Mexico. It is the perfect place to have young.

Pregnant females find shallow **lagoons**. The lagoons are warm. They are also safe from sharks and other **predators**.

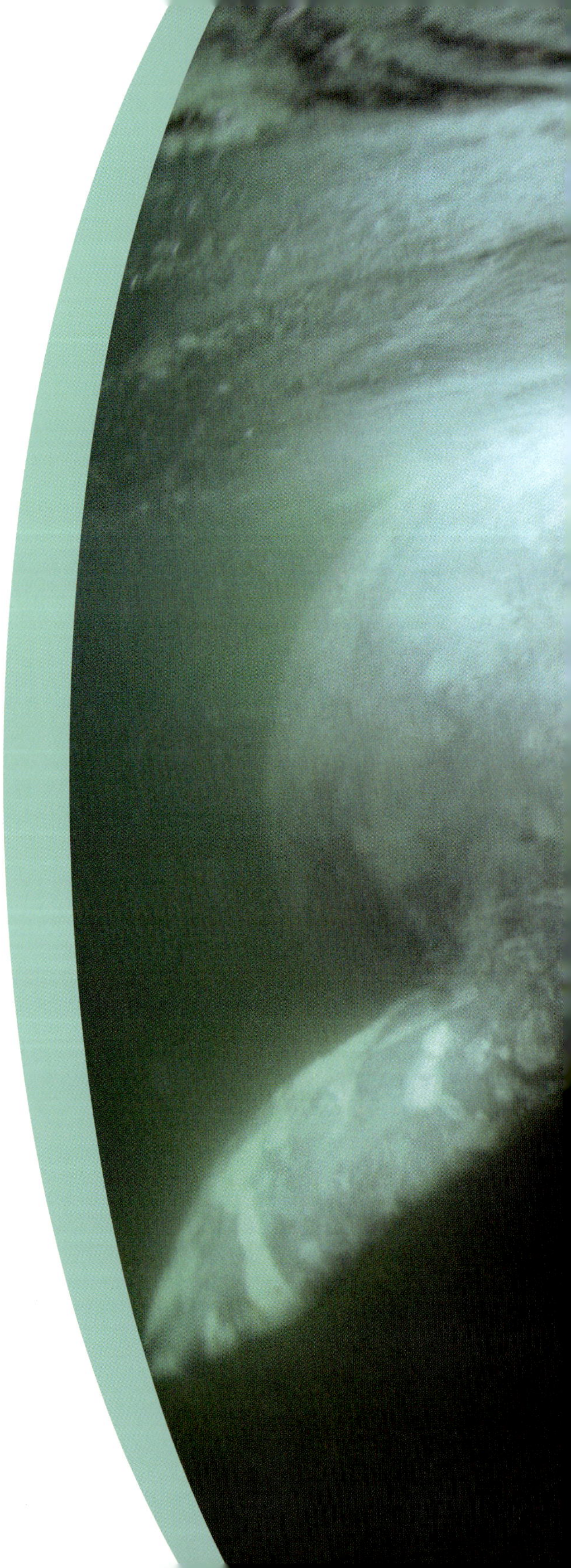

Females give birth to one calf at a time. Calves are around 13 feet (4 m) long when they are born. They rely on their mothers for milk.

Back Home to Eat

In springtime, the **migration** home to Alaska begins. Males and newly pregnant females are the first to move north.

New mothers and calves stay for a month or two longer. Calves need to gain lots of **blubber** before the long journey.

It is important to make it back to Alaska. This is where the gray whales eat. They must gain lots of weight to prepare for the next **migration** south.

Gray Whale Migration Route

Summer Home   Winter Home   ---- Route

Glossary

blubber – the layer of fat beneath the skin of whales and other large sea mammals.

lagoon – a shallow body of salt water by the sea.

mammal – a warm-blooded animal with fur or hair on its skin and a skeleton inside its body. Mammal mothers make milk to feed their young.

migrate – to move from one place to another for food, weather, or other important reasons.

predator – an animal that hunts other animals for food.

Index

Canada Goose Migration

by Grace Hansen

Abdo
ANIMAL MIGRATION
Kids

Abdo Kids Jumbo is an Imprint of Abdo Kids
abdobooks.com

abdobooks.com

Published by Abdo Kids, a division of ABDO, P.O. Box 398166, Minneapolis, Minnesota 55439.

Printed in the United States of America, North Mankato, Minnesota.

052020

092020

THIS BOOK CONTAINS RECYCLED MATERIALS

Photo Credits: iStock, Shutterstock

Production Contributors: Teddy Borth, Jennie Forsberg, Grace Hansen
Design Contributors: Dorothy Toth, Pakou Moua

Library of Congress Control Number: 2019956466

Publisher's Cataloging-in-Publication Data

Names: Hansen, Grace, author.

Title: Canada goose migration / by Grace Hansen

Description: Minneapolis, Minnesota : Abdo Kids, 2021 | Series: Animal migration | Includes online resources and index.

Identifiers: ISBN 9781098202293 (lib. bdg.) | ISBN 9781098203276 (ebook) | ISBN 9781098203764 (Read-to-Me ebook)

Subjects: LCSH: Canada goose--Juvenile literature. | Canada goose--Behavior--Juvenile literature. | Flyways--Juvenile literature. | Animal migration--Juvenile literature. | Animal migration--Climatic factors--Juvenile literature.

Classification: DDC 598.252--dc23

Table of Contents

Canada Geese

Canada geese live all over North America. They got their name because they were often seen flying toward Canada. Many of them live in Canada in the summer months.

Canada geese can be found in many different habitats. But they are always found near water when nesting.

Canada geese most often feed on plants in fields. They also eat water plants. Sometimes, they'll eat insects and other small animals.

Flying in Formation

Food is the main reason Canada geese **migrate**. In wintertime in Canada and the northern United States, fields are covered in snow. Ponds and lakes are frozen. And insects are nowhere to be found.

In fall, Canada geese fly south in a **V formation**. Geese that live in northern Canada often **migrate** the farthest.

Most land in the southern United States. Others will fly all the way to the Gulf of Mexico. And others will end up in northern Mexico.

The geese spend the winter

in their southern homes.

Their days are filled with

eating and resting.

Returning Home

In the spring, they are ready to return home and **mate**. Canada geese lay eggs between February and April. The eggs hatch after 28 to 30 days.

The **goslings** are taken to water. Their parents teach them to feed. Come fall, they will be strong enough to fly south for the winter.

Canada Goose Migration Routes

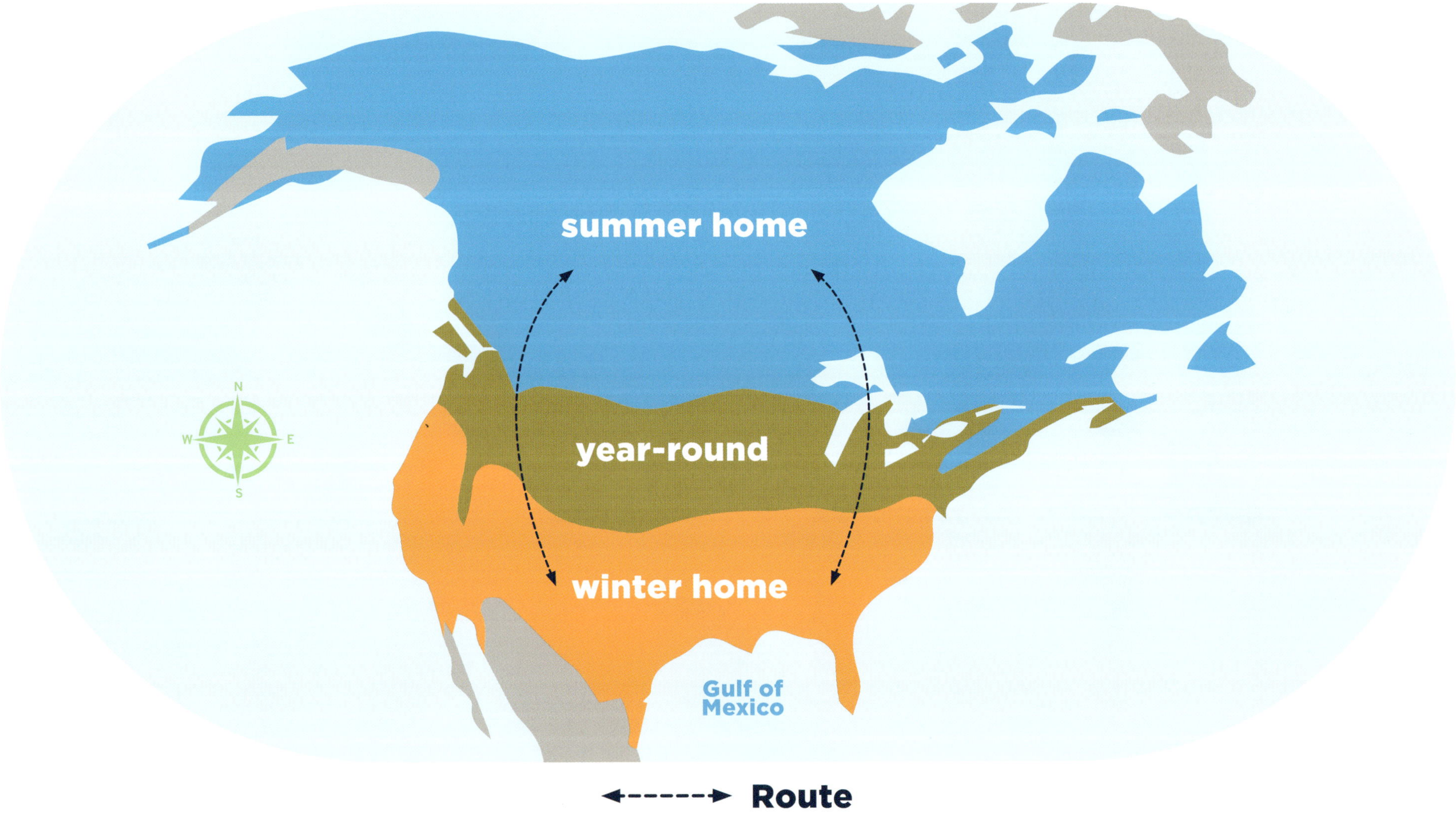

Glossary

gosling – a very young goose.

mate – to come together to have offspring.

migrate – to move from one place to another for food, weather, or other important reasons.

V formation – the symmetric v-shaped flight formation of geese that helps save energy over long migratory routes.

Index

Arctic Tern Migration

by Grace Hansen

Abdo Kids
ANIMAL MIGRATION

Abdo Kids Jumbo is an Imprint of Abdo Kids
abdobooks.com

abdobooks.com

Published by Abdo Kids, a division of ABDO, P.O. Box 398166, Minneapolis, Minnesota 55439.

Printed in the United States of America, North Mankato, Minnesota.

052020

092020

THIS BOOK CONTAINS RECYCLED MATERIALS

Photo Credits: iStock, National Geographic Image Collection, Shutterstock

Production Contributors: Teddy Borth, Jennie Forsberg, Grace Hansen
Design Contributors: Dorothy Toth, Pakou Moua

Library of Congress Control Number: 2019956472

Publisher's Cataloging-in-Publication Data

Names: Hansen, Grace, author.

Title: Arctic tern migration / by Grace Hansen

Description: Minneapolis, Minnesota : Abdo Kids, 2021 | Series: Animal migration | Includes online resources and index.

Identifiers: ISBN 9781098202286 (lib. bdg.) | ISBN 9781098203269 (ebook) | ISBN 9781098203757 (Read-to-Me ebook)

Subjects: LCSH: Arctic tern--Juvenile literature. | Birds--Behavior--Juvenile literature. | Flyways--Juvenile literature. | Animal migration--Juvenile literature. | Animal migration--Climatic factors--Juvenile literature.

Classification: DDC 598.252--dc23

Table of Contents

Arctic Terns

The Arctic tern gets its name from where it is born.

5

Arctic terns are amazing little birds. They have the longest **migrations** of any animal.

Arctic terns **breed** across the Arctic. They nest in **colonies** and often near coasts.

Arctic terns lay 1 to 3 eggs. After they hatch, parents feed the chicks for about a month. Soon, the chicks will learn to **plunge-dive** for food.

The Longest Migration

Arctic terns spend two to three months in their nesting areas. The young grow stronger in that time. In August and September, they begin a very long journey south to **Antarctica**.

Arctic
N
W
E
S
Antarctica

Arctic terns fly up to 57,000 miles (92,000 km) each year! Like most animals, they **migrate** to find food. They are also avoiding the harsh Arctic winters.

Arctic terns stay in **Antarctica** for up to 5 months. They spend time feeding in the Antarctic waters.

Their **migrations** to and from their winter home include stops. They eat and rest during these stops. This gives them energy for their long flights.

Coming Home

Arctic terns arrive home in May or June. Most of them return to the same place each year.

Arctic Tern Migration Routes

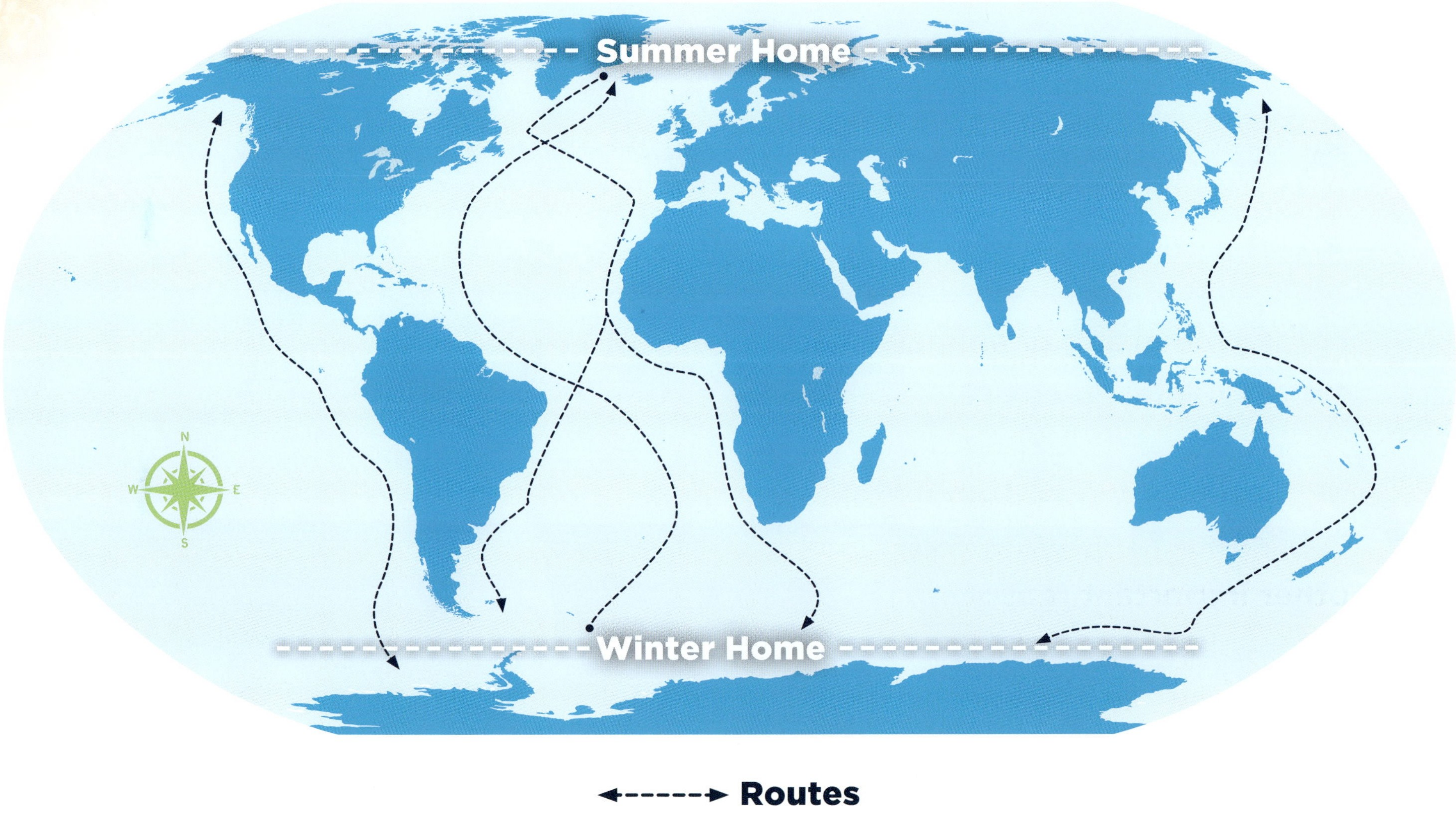

Glossary

Antarctica – the continent that surrounds the South Pole.

breed – to produce young.

colony – a group of animals of the same type living closely together.

migrate – to move from one place to another for food, weather, or other important reasons.

migration – the act or process of migrating.

plunge-diving – a hunting method used by seabirds to catch fish and other water animals.

Index

Caribou Migration

by Grace Hansen

Abdo ANIMAL MIGRATION Kids

Abdo Kids Jumbo is an Imprint of Abdo Kids
abdobooks.com

abdobooks.com

Published by Abdo Kids, a division of ABDO, P.O. Box 398166, Minneapolis, Minnesota 55439.

Printed in the United States of America, North Mankato, Minnesota.

052020

092020

THIS BOOK CONTAINS RECYCLED MATERIALS

Photo Credits: Alamy, iStock, National Geographic Image Collection, Shutterstock

Production Contributors: Teddy Borth, Jennie Forsberg, Grace Hansen
Design Contributors: Dorothy Toth, Pakou Moua

Library of Congress Control Number: 2019956467

Publisher's Cataloging-in-Publication Data

Names: Hansen, Grace, author.

Title: Caribou migration / by Grace Hansen

Description: Minneapolis, Minnesota : Abdo Kids, 2021 | Series: Animal migration | Includes online resources and index.

Identifiers: ISBN 9781098202309 (lib. bdg.) | ISBN 9781098203283 (ebook) | ISBN 9781098203771 (Read-to-Me ebook)

Subjects: LCSH: Caribou--Juvenile literature. | Caribou--Behavior--Juvenile literature. | Reindeer—Behavior--Juvenile literature. | Animal migration--Juvenile literature. | Animal migration--Climatic factors--Juvenile literature.

Classification: DDC 599.658--dc23

Table of Contents

Caribou

Caribou are mainly found in Alaska and Canada. They live in the **tundra** and **taiga** areas.

Caribou are built to survive in cold and harsh conditions. However, their greatest means of survival is **migration**.

Great Group Migration

Caribou **migrate** between summer and winter ranges. They are almost always on the move. Caribou herds can travel up to 3,000 miles (4,800 km) a year.

Their summer range has **nutritious** food. Eating these plants allows mothers to make rich milk. This helps the calves grow faster and stronger.

The summer range also has fewer **predators** and insects. It is an ideal place for raising young.

However, the summer range is harsh in the winter months. Strong winds and very cold temperatures make it unlivable. So the caribou move south between August and October.

Caribou's winter range has more food and is not as cold. The herd will remain there until late March.

Back to the Summer Home

In early April, they will begin their journey north again. Pregnant females start moving first.

In early June, mothers give birth. The rest of the herd makes it back to the summer grounds by mid-July. Soon, their **migration** south will begin again.

Western Arctic Caribou Herd Migration Route

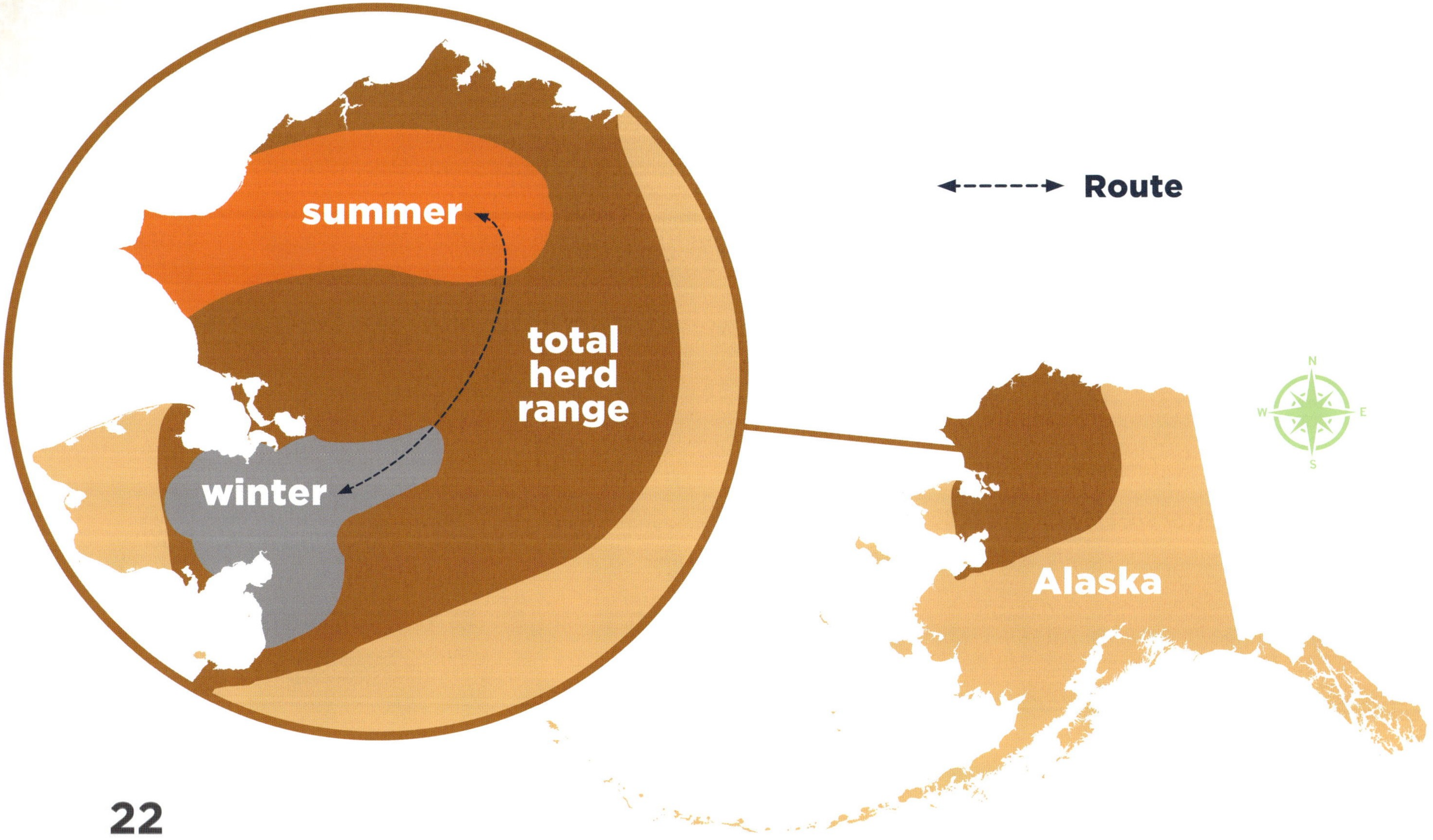

Glossary

migrate – to move from one place to another for food, weather, or other important reasons.

migration – the act or process of migrating.

nutritious – having a lot of vitamins, minerals, or other nutrients necessary to grow or stay strong.

predator – an animal that hunts other animals for food.

taiga – the strip of subarctic evergreen forest that covers much of the northern parts of North America, Europe, and Asia.

tundra – one of the huge plains in the arctic regions of North America, Europe, and Asia. Trees do not grow on tundra.

Index

abdobooks.com

Published by Abdo Kids, a division of ABDO, P.O. Box 398166, Minneapolis, Minnesota 55439.

Printed in the United States of America, North Mankato, Minnesota.

052020

092020

THIS BOOK CONTAINS RECYCLED MATERIALS

Photo Credits: Alamy, iStock, Minden Pictures, Shutterstock

Production Contributors: Teddy Borth, Jennie Forsberg, Grace Hansen
Design Contributors: Dorothy Toth, Pakou Moua

Library of Congress Control Number: 2019956468

Publisher's Cataloging-in-Publication Data

Names: Hansen, Grace, author.

Title: Emperor penguin migration / by Grace Hansen

Description: Minneapolis, Minnesota : Abdo Kids, 2021 | Series: Animal migration | Includes online resources and index.

Identifiers: ISBN 9781098202323 (lib. bdg.) | ISBN 9781098203306 (ebook) | ISBN 9781098203795 (Read-to-Me ebook)

Subjects: LCSH: Penguins--Juvenile literature. | Emperor penguin--Behavior--Juvenile literature. | Animal migration--Juvenile literature. | Animal migration--Climatic factors--Juvenile literature.

Classification: DDC 598.47--dc23

Table of Contents

Emperor Penguins

Emperor penguins live in **Antarctica**. It is the coldest **continent** on Earth.

Emperor penguins live near the coast. They stay close to the water. They hunt in the water.

The March of the Emperor Penguins

Summer in **Antarctica** lasts from December until March. In March, emperor penguins **migrate** inland. It is time to go to their nesting areas.

land
nest
migrate
sea
food

The nesting area is usually around 50 miles (80 km) inland. Each female lays one egg. She passes the egg to the male. He keeps it warm and safe.

Female emperor penguins return to the ocean. They feed for the winter.

land
nest
females
sea
food

Protecting the Young

Winter in **Antarctica** is harsh. The males huddle together. They cannot eat. They must protect the eggs.

The eggs begin to hatch in July. Females return to the nesting grounds. Now it is their turn to watch over the young.

land
sea
nest
females
food

The thin males are ready for a big meal after a long winter. They make their way back to the ocean. Later, males and females will take turns returning to the ocean.

land
sea
nest
males
food

In springtime, the chicks begin to molt. They grow their **waterproof** feathers. The chicks will be mature in 4 to 5 years. Then they will **migrate** like their parents.

Emperor Penguin Migration Route

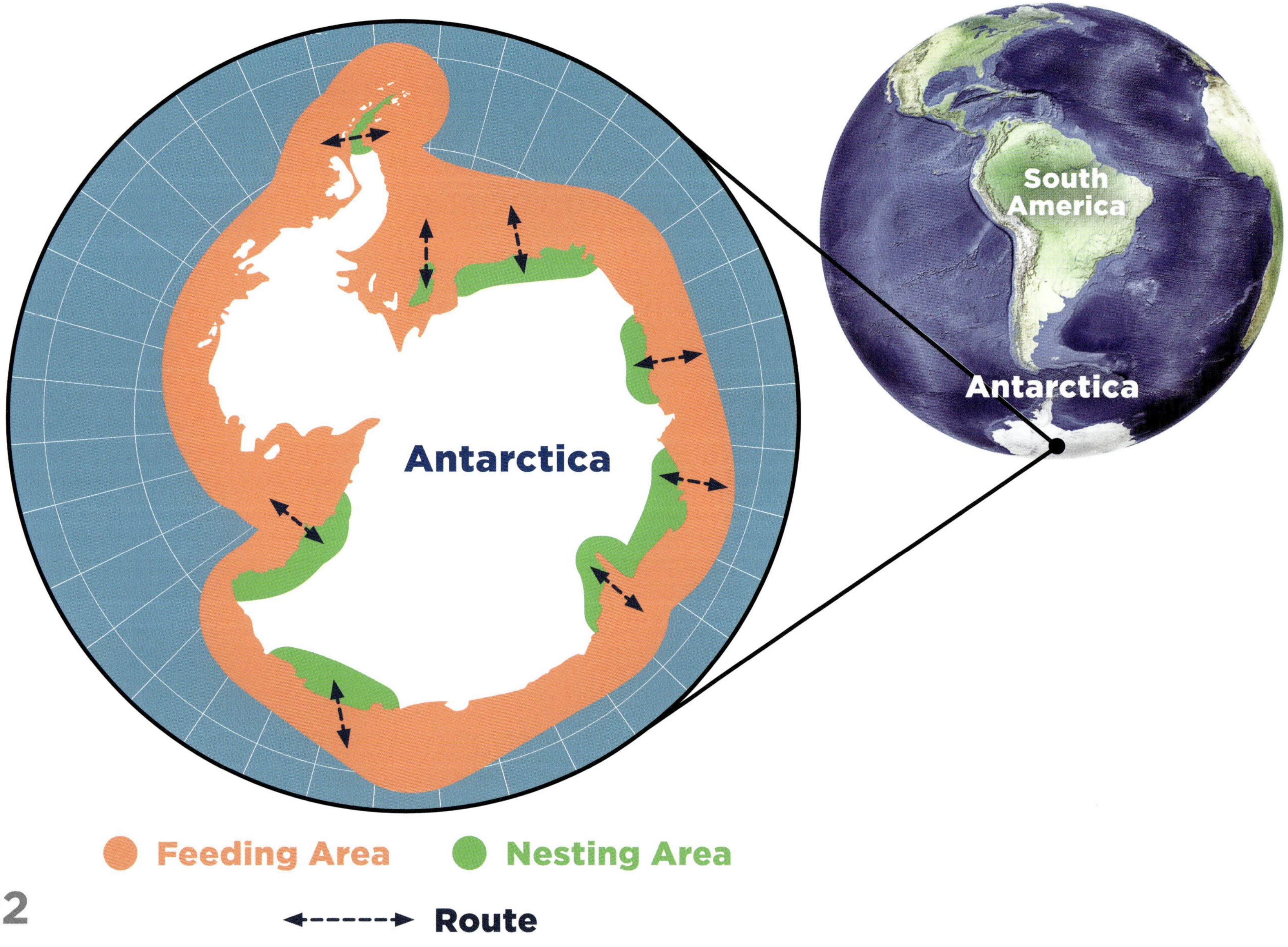

Glossary

Antarctica – the continent that surrounds the South Pole.

continent – one of Earth's seven major areas of land. The continents are Africa, Antarctica, Asia, Australia, Europe, North America, and South America.

migrate – to move from one place to another for food, weather, or other important reasons.

waterproof – not letting water through.

Index

Dragonfly Migration

by Grace Hansen

Abdo
ANIMAL MIGRATION
Kids

Abdo Kids Jumbo is an Imprint of Abdo Kids
abdobooks.com

abdobooks.com

Published by Abdo Kids, a division of ABDO, P.O. Box 398166, Minneapolis, Minnesota 55439.

Printed in the United States of America, North Mankato, Minnesota.

052020

092020

THIS BOOK CONTAINS RECYCLED MATERIALS

Photo Credits: Alamy, iStock, Shutterstock

Production Contributors: Teddy Borth, Jennie Forsberg, Grace Hansen
Design Contributors: Dorothy Toth, Pakou Moua

Library of Congress Control Number: 2019956493

Publisher's Cataloging-in-Publication Data

Names: Hansen, Grace, author.

Title: Dragonfly migration / by Grace Hansen

Description: Minneapolis, Minnesota : Abdo Kids, 2021 | Series: Animal migration | Includes online resources and index.

Identifiers: ISBN 9781098202316 (lib. bdg.) | ISBN 9781098203290 (ebook) | ISBN 9781098203788 (Read-to-Me ebook)

Subjects: LCSH: Dragonflies--Juvenile literature. | Insects--Behavior--Juvenile literature. | Animal migration--Juvenile literature. | Animal migration--Climatic factors--Juvenile literature.

Classification: DDC 595.7052--dc23

Table of Contents

Dragonflies

Dragonflies can be found all over the world. Some **species** travel great distances to lay eggs.

Green Darner Migration

Green darners of North America **migrate** each spring and fall. They can travel up to 900 miles (1,448 km). They migrate from Canada to the Gulf of Mexico.

N
W
E
S
Canada
United States
Gulf of Mexico
Mexico

It takes several **generations** to **migrate** this far. In early spring, the green darner leaves its winter home. It flies around 400 miles (644 km) north.

The group lands and lays eggs. Then they die. The eggs hatch. The young dragonflies continue their journey north.

In September, the dragonflies fly south again. They also lay eggs and die. The cycle continues.

Globe Skimmer Migration

A more impressive **migration** happens on the other side of the world. The globe skimmer makes up to an 11,000-mile (18,000 km) journey. This is the farthest migration of any insect on Earth.

Africa
India
Maldives

Globe skimmers of India follow the rainy weather that moves west. They do this because dragonflies need water to lay their eggs.

Many globe skimmers stop in the **Maldives** to lay eggs. Then they keep moving west across the Indian Ocean between July and December.

In time, the dragonflies will make it to Africa. Scientists believe the tiny insects are able to do this by riding the winds. They use their large wings to **glide** along.

Globe Skimmer Migration Route

Glossary

generation – a group of living things that were born around the same time.

glide – to move smoothly and without effort.

Maldives – an island country in the Indian Ocean that lies southwest of Sri Lanka. It is made up of about 2,000 islands. Its capital is Malé.

migrate – to move from one place to another for food, weather, or other important reasons.

species – a group of living things that look very much alike and can have young with one another.

Emperor Penguin Migration

by Grace Hansen

Abdo
ANIMAL MIGRATION
Kids

Abdo Kids Jumbo is an Imprint of Abdo Kids
abdobooks.com

Index